My Body

My Bones

Sally Hewitt

QEB Publishing

Copyright © QEB Publishing 2008
First published in the USA in 2008 by
QEB Publishing, Inc
23602 La Cadena Drive
Laguna Hills, CA 92653

www.qeb-publishing.com

Library of Congress Control Number:
2008011705

ISBN 978 1 59566 552 2

Printed and bound in China

Author Sally Hewitt

Consultant Terry Jennings
Project Editor Judith Millidge
Designer Kim Hall
Picture Researcher Claudia Tate
Illustrator Chris Davidson

Publisher Steve Evans
Creative Director Zeta Davies

Picture credits

Key: t = top, b = bottom, m = middle,
l = left, r = right

Alamy Jim Zuckerman 7, Jupiterimages-Polka Dot 17t
Corbis Jennie Woodcock-Reflections Photolibrary 19r,
Virgo Productions-Zefa 19l
Getty Images Barbara Peacock 17t
Shutterstock Irina Klebanova 5b, Teodor Ostojic 5t,
Elena Elisseeva 6, Roberto Kylio 8, Olga Lyubkina 8,
Julian Rovagnati 8, Kivrins Anatolijs 9b, Graca
Victoria 9t, Philip Lange 10t, Serghei Starus 10b, George
P Choma 11, Ariusz Nawrocki 12, Andresr 13tl, Gelpi 13m,
Kameel4u 13tr, Cindy Minear 14, Jiang Dao Hua 15,
JoLin 21b

Words in bold are
explained in the glossary
on page 22.

Contents

What is your skeleton?

Your skeleton is like a strong frame. It gives your body its **shape**, holds you upright, and lets you move. It **protects** soft parts of your body, such as your heart and lungs.

Your skeleton is made up of bones of different shapes and sizes. Each bone has a job to do.

4

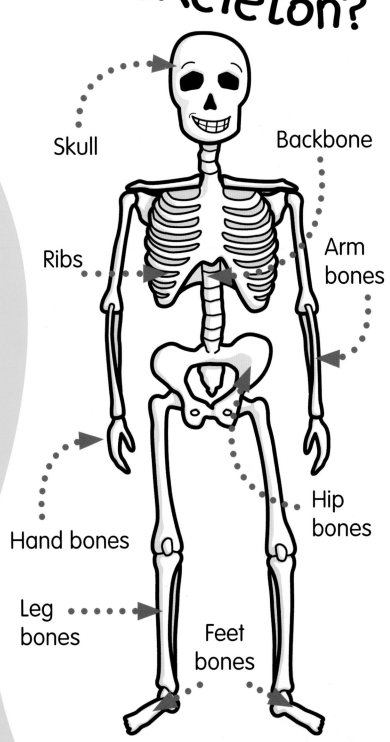

Skull

Backbone

Ribs

Arm bones

Hand bones

Hip bones

Leg bones

Feet bones

Your body is **alive** and growing, and so are your bones. As you grow older, your bones become harder and stronger. By the time you are fully grown, you will have 206 bones.

Activity

Which of your bones can you feel through your skin?

Can you feel the top of the bone in your upper arm? Your ribs?

5

Your bones

Your bones need to be strong and light. Bones are light enough to let you jump, and strong enough not to break when you land.

Marrow

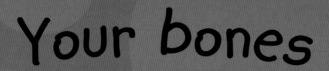

Hard bone

Spongy bone

The outside layer of a bone is hard, and the middle layer is like a sponge. In the center of many bones is a jelly called marrow.

Even though bones are very strong, they sometimes break. Bones are amazing! They can mend themselves and become just as strong again.

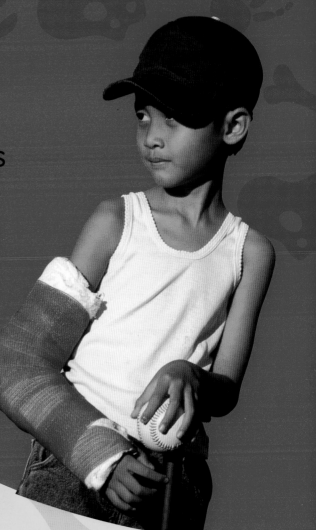

It usually takes about six weeks for a broken bone to mend.

If you break your arm, you go to hospital. A doctor sets your broken bone, and your arm is put in a plaster cast to hold the bone in place. A sling **supports** your arm while it heals.

Healthy bones

Just like the rest of your body, your bones need plenty of good food and **exercise**, as well as rest and sleep.

Milk, eggs, cheese, and yogurt, tinned salmon and sardines, as well as leafy, green vegetables all help to keep your bones strong and healthy.

Whatever exercise you enjoy, such as running, dancing, or ball games, will keep you active and help your bones to grow strong.

Do something active every day.

Wear a helmet when you ride a bicycle to protect your skull. Wear pads to protect your knees and elbows when you skate.

You can have fun and look after your bones!

Joints

Your bones join together at places called **joints**. Most of the joints in your skeleton can move.

If you didn't have joints, you would be as stiff as a statue.

Activity

Move around.
Can you work out which
of your joints move?
What kind of movements
can they make?

Your joints move in different ways. You have "ball-and-socket" joints, where your arms join your shoulders and where your legs join your hips. These joints let your arms and legs move round in a circle.

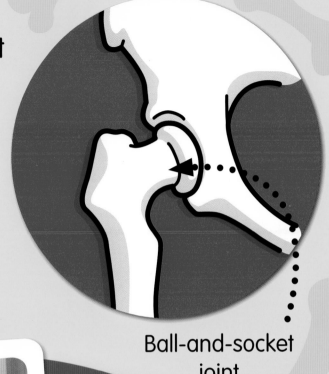

Ball-and-socket joint

Elbows and knees are "hinge" joints. They move backward and forward like the hinges on a door.

Your skull

Your skull is made up of several bones. It is very strong. Its most important job is to protect your brain. Feel the shape of your skull. It has two holes for your eyes. Your jaw opens and closes when you talk and also when you eat.

The top of your skull is exactly the right shape and size to cover and protect your brain.

The bones in your skull give your face its shape. We all have a forehead, eyes, nose, a mouth, and a chin. Everyone looks just a bit different so we can recognize each other easily.

It would be very confusing if we all looked exactly the same.

Activity

Look in the mirror and draw a picture of your face. Then, draw your friend's face. Which parts of the drawings look the same and which look different?

13

Your backbone

Your backbone, or "spine," runs right down the middle of your back. It is made up of 26 small bones. If it were made of just one long bone, you would not be able to bend or twist.

Spine

Activity

Bend your knees, curl your back, and touch your toes, then stand up again. Feel your backbone bend and straighten up again.

14

Your backbone holds you upright. If you stand, walk, and sit with a straight back, your spine supports your whole body. If you let your back bend while you are standing or sitting, you will soon start to ache all over.

Gymnasts hold their back straight to help them balance.

15

Your ribs

Your ribs are shaped like a cage. They protect your heart, which pumps blood around your body, and your lungs, which you use for breathing.

You have 12 pairs of ribs. They are fixed to your backbone. The top seven pairs of ribs are fixed to your breastbone at the front.

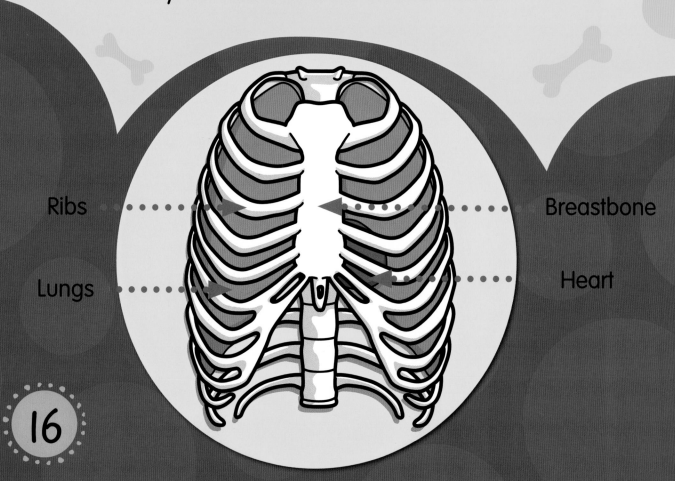

Ribs .... Breastbone

Lungs .... Heart

You can feel your ribs and you can probably see the shape of them through your skin, too.
The bottom two pairs of ribs are only fixed at the back so they can move more easily when you breathe in and out.

Activity

Take a deep breath. Your lungs will fill up with air just like this balloon.

Arms and hands

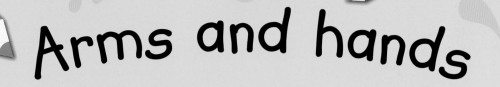

You use your arms and hands to grip and to pick things up, write, and draw, and play with toys!

Each arm, wrist, and hand is made up of 30 bones, which help you make all these different movements.

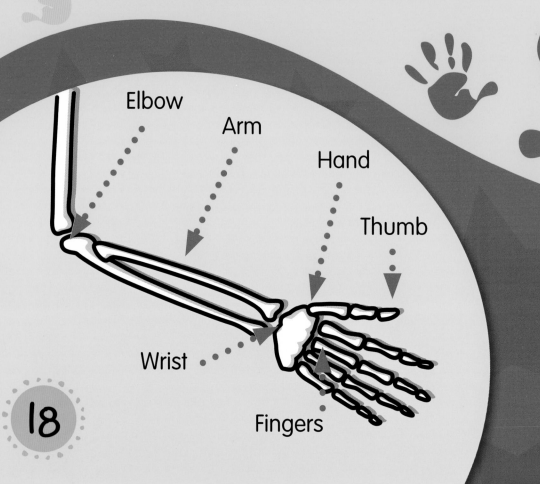

Elbow

Arm

Hand

Thumb

Wrist

Fingers

18

The bone in the top of your arm is strong and thick. You have two thinner bones in the bottom of your arm and 27 bones in your hand and wrist!

Lots of little bones in your fingers help you make small movements.

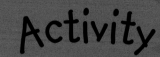

Activity

Make a model with modeling clay. Notice how you move all the bones in your arms and hands.

19

Legs and feet

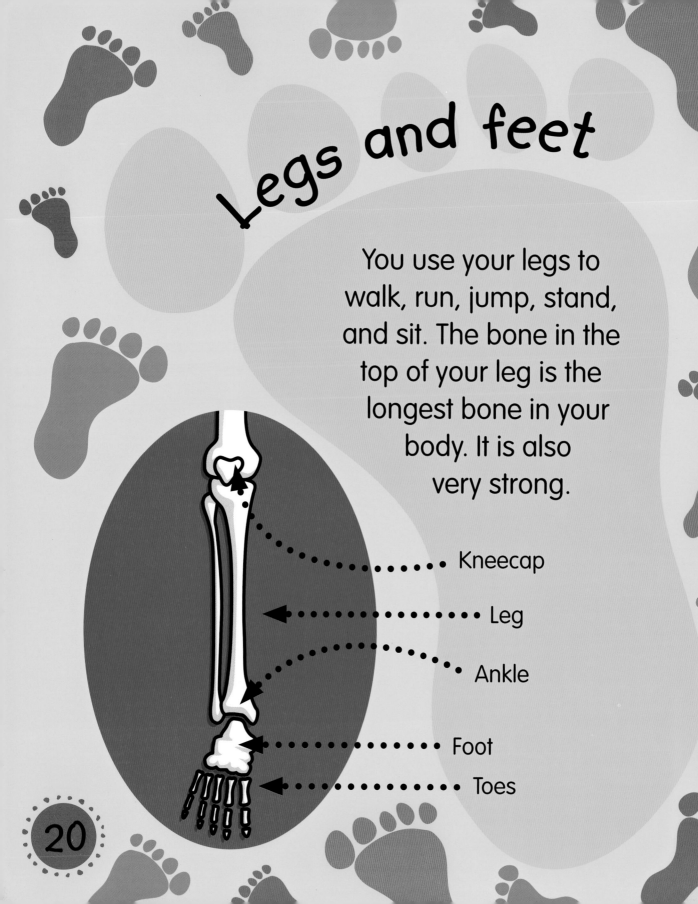

You use your legs to walk, run, jump, stand, and sit. The bone in the top of your leg is the longest bone in your body. It is also very strong.

Kneecap

Leg

Ankle

Foot

Toes

20

A bone called the kneecap protects your knee joint. Children often cut and bruise their knees, so kneecaps have an important job to do!

Have you ever cut or bruised your knee?

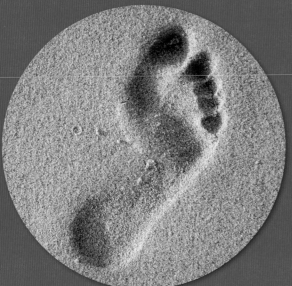

It is fun to make footprints on a sandy beach. You can make footprints at home, too!

Activity

Put some dark paper in a tray and sprinkle flour on top of it. Stand in the flour. Now carefully step out without smudging the flour. Can you see how the bones in your foot spread out to help you stand?

21

Glossary

Alive
You are alive, and so are plants and animals. Things that are alive grow, move, eat, and can sense what is going on around them.

Bone
Bones are strong and light. The 206 bones in your body are joined together to make up your skeleton.

Exercise
Exercise is moving about, for example running, swimming, jumping, stretching, and skipping. Exercise helps to keep your body strong and healthy.

Joint
"Joint" is the name given to a part of the body where two bones meet. Most of your joints can move. Your elbows and knees are joints.

Protect
"Protect" means to keep something safe from being hurt. Your skull protects your brain.

Shape
Everything has a shape. For example, a ball is a round shape. Your skeleton gives your body its shape.

Support
"Support" means to hold something upright or stop it from falling.

Notes for parents and teachers

1. Have fun drawing a skeleton together. Look at the picture on page 4 to help you. Talk about the shape of the bones you are drawing and feel them under your skin. When you have drawn the skeleton, stick it onto some card and cut it out. Now cut it into sections: head, body, arms, and legs. You can put the sections back together using paper fasteners to make a skeleton with a moving head and limbs.

2. Visit a museum with skeletons on display or look at a book with pictures of human, animal, or even dinosaur skeletons. Notice that they all have skulls and backbones. Discuss the differences in the shapes of the skeletons and the size of the bones.

3. Look at worms, slugs, and snails, which do not have internal skeletons to support them. Notice how they move without bones and joints.

4. Talk about bones being strong and light. Look at different bones whenever you get the chance, for example, cooked chicken, fish, and beef bones. Notice the differences between them and work out which part of the body they come from. (It is best if the bones are handled only by an adult.)

5. Find all the places in your body that bend and name the joints. You could play a game of "Simon says," changing the instructions to: "Simon says bend your elbow," (or wrist, knee, etc.). Sit down if you bend the wrong joint!

Index